stories
from my
grandparent

stories
from my
grandparent

An Heirloom Journal
for Your Grandchild

Susan Adcox

FAMILY
TREE
BOOKS

Cincinnati, Ohio
shopfamilytree.com

Introduction

We are all writers in the sense that we shape the narratives of our lives. With this book, you have the opportunity to put down in words the life story that you have already written. Most importantly, you are recording your story for a very special audience: a grandchild.

Why should you write down your story? Human memories are mutable. You can't rely on others to remember the details of your life. Besides, this book can spark many lovely conversations between you and your grandchild. And someday, when you are gone, this little book will still be around, creating an eternal bond between you and your grandchild.

No one's life has been free of pain and sadness, but I hope that you'll create a book that will be pleasant and inspirational for your grandchild, so that he or she will want to read it over and over. You don't have to ignore the hard times; indeed some of the questions address the trials of life. But if you have bitterness or unresolved conflicts, I would suggest that you not put them in writing but rather make the decision about whether to share them at a later date.

If the preceding makes writing this book feel like a solemn undertaking, remember that children love to laugh. Put in some funny stories. More advice:

- Don't stress about the task. Perfection is impossible. What's more, it's not even desirable.
- Don't worry about your handwriting. It will make the book more precious to your grandchild.
- If you make a mistake, cross it out.
- When the prompts don't fit your life, adapt them. Every grandparent's life has followed a slightly different trajectory.
- If prompted to write about something that doesn't apply to you, skip it, or use the space to write about something else.
- Don't get sidetracked by too much research. This book is designed as a record of your life as you remember it.

With a little perseverance, you'll create a gift for your grandchild that's a lot like you: imperfect, individualistic and always interesting.

Use photo corners or
double-sided tape to affix photo.

To My Grandchild

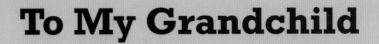

This is my story, and all of it is true, or at least recorded to the best of my memory. I am writing it down for you, my grandchild, because we have a connection that is so precious to me in the present but that I also want to last into infinity.

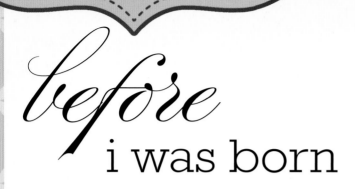

before i was born

If I really wanted to start at the beginning, I would have to go back hundreds of years in time and tell you about our ancestors. I would love to have that conversation some day, but this isn't that kind of book.

This story begins with a man named ...., my father, and a woman named ...., my mother. They were my parents and your great-grandparents, and I want to tell you what they were like when they were young.

My Father

Use photo corners or
double-sided tape to affix photo.

From photographs and from my own early memories, this is what my father looked like:

I know this about his family history and cultural heritage:

I know where he grew up and a bit about his early life:

As a young man, my father had these personality traits:

My Mother

Use photo corners or double-sided tape to affix photo.

From photographs and from my own early memories, this is what my mother looked like:

_____

_____

_____

I know this about her family history and cultural heritage:

_____

_____

_____

_____

I know where she grew up and a bit about her early life:

_____

_____

_____

_____

As a young woman, my mother had these personality traits:

_____

_____

_____

_____

Two interesting people, but if they had never come together, there would be no "me." This is what I've been told about how they met and courted and about their marriage:

....

....

....

....

An important step in understanding your ancestors is knowing something about how they looked at the world. This is what I know about my parents' religious backgrounds and beliefs:

....

....

....

I wasn't yet on the scene, but this is what I've been told about my parent's early life together. (What fun! What challenges!):

....

....

....

my story begins

**Now we're getting to the good part,
where I arrive on the scene.**

I was born on ...., and the location was ....

....

When I was born, ... was the President of the United States.

Besides my birth, some other important events occurred in the nation and in the world that year:

....

....

"How much did the baby weigh? Who does the baby look like?" That's what everyone wanted to know

about me. Here are the answers. I weighed ....

From the pictures that I have seen, this is how I would describe myself as a newborn:

....

....

14

Use photo corners or double-sided tape to affix photo.

These are the names I was given:

My parents had this to say about my name:

15

Later, I would be known by these nicknames:

....

....

....

....

....

My parents loved me, of course, but sometimes I could be a handful. This is what I've been told about myself as a baby:

....

....

....

....

....

Early Memories

Now we get to the good part of the story, the parts I can remember.

Although our parents shape our early years, we are also influenced by the places where we live. These are my memories of my early homes:

....

....

....

 Use photo corners or double-sided tape to affix photo.

Besides taking care of me, my parents were also busy with these careers and activities:

Some say that birth order is really important to a child, but being loved is definitely more important. I was the................................child in a family of................................children.

This is how I felt about my position in the family:

Besides parents, brothers and sisters are probably the most important people in a child's life. Here's a bit about my siblings:

....

....

....

....

 Use photo corners or
double-sided tape to affix photo.

As a grandparent, I've been influenced by my memories of my own grandparents. Here's what I remember about my grandparents on my mother's side:

 Use photo corners or double-sided tape to affix photo.

Here's what I remember about my grandparents on my father's side.

 Use photo corners or
double-sided tape to affix photo.

Pets can be special friends to little ones. Meet some of my childhood buddies:

_____

_____

_____

_____

_____

_____

Although I was mostly happy and healthy, I did have these sicknesses and health issues:

_____

_____

_____

_____

_____

_____

My Daily Life

**Although my life was very different from your life, dear grandchild,
I had favorite ways of spending my days, just as you do.**

I spent many hours playing with these favorite toys:

....

....

Just as in our world today, occasionally a certain toy became very popular. Everyone wanted one!
These were some of the popular toys of my youth:

....

....

We didn't have video games, but I enjoyed these favorite board games and card games:

....

....

Television sets were not the fancy devices that they are today. We sat in front of a small box that
received only a few channels, but we still found programs that delighted and amused us. My favorite
programs and performers were:

....

....

Going to the movies was a real treat. We saw movies in indoor theaters or outdoor drive-ins. This is what I remember about going to the movies with family and friends:

I wonder if you've ever seen some of my favorite movies from my childhood? Here are a few that stand out in my memory:

Later, when I became a teenager, music would rule my world, but it was important in my childhood as well. Listening to music involved either the radio or something called a record player. Of course, some families were lucky enough to have musical performers in the family. Here's how my family enjoyed music and the types of music we preferred:

When I was a child, children were expected to play outside much of the time, which was fine with us. My playmates and I enjoyed these outdoor activities:

Sports are really important to some families, both the playing of sports and the watching of sports. This is how my family felt about sports:

Many of my childhood memories involve food, and it was mostly cooked at home. People didn't go to restaurants very often. Mmmmm. These were my home-cooked favorites:

Children were commonly expected to clean their plates, which could be a problem for me when these foods were on my plate:

Here's a funny little story for you about me and food:

Besides nourishing my body with food, my family was careful to nourish my spiritual being. We went to worship services:

....

....

I was encouraged to pray:

....

....

My spiritual being was recognized with these ceremonies:

....

....

I had favorite scriptures and sacred stories:

....

....

Elementary School Memories

Starting to school was an event that my friends and I happily looked forward to. We were growing up and getting big! Still, there were some worries mixed in. We would miss our carefree lives.

My school career began at .... School, located in

....

I also attended these other elementary schools:

....

....

A person's first teacher in kindergarten or first grade plays many parts: substitute parent, teacher, cheerleader and keeper of order in the classroom. Here's what I remember about my first teacher(s):

....

....

....

On a typical school day, I would have been wearing this outfit:

....

....

....

Even though it has been many years, the names and faces of some of my classmates are engraved on my memory. I especially remember the person I considered my best friend:

_____

_____

_____

_____

Recess was every kid's favorite part of the day. This is what we did at recess:

_____

_____

_____

In our classroom, we had real chalkboards. We had spelling bees and go-to-the-board drills, but no computers. Here's what I remember about my first classroom and how we learned:

_____

_____

_____

How magical it was when I could look at letters on a page and understand what they meant! Here's what I remember about learning to read:

I will never forget this book that I read when I was very young:

I was usually a good kid, but I do remember getting in trouble once or twice:

School picture day was a big event. This is what the camera revealed when it was pointed at me:

 Use photo corners or
double-sided tape to affix photo.

I also remember report card days. I know you are eager to know if I made good grades. Here's all I'm going to tell you about that:

When I was in elementary school, someone was always asking, "What do you want to be when you grow up?" This was my answer:

Time Outside of School

Even though most of us secretly enjoyed school, we also looked forward to free time after school, on the weekend and during the summer.

I spent my time after school and my weekends enjoying these activities:

....

....

....

When I was a kid, a lot of sports were played informally, on a vacant lot or other open spot. Of course, organized sports such as Little League existed as well. Here are the sports I enjoyed and how we played them:

....

....

....

Organizations such as 4-H and Scouts enriched the lives of many kids. I belonged to these organizations and enjoyed these activities:

....

....

....

These church organizations and activities were also an important part of my life:

Once we reached a certain age, we enjoyed sleepovers and slumber parties. We had great fun, although it was hard to keep my eyes open the next day. I'll never forget these sleepover pals and the things we used to do:

Summers held lots of long, lazy days, but summer was also the time for going to camp:

Family Time

Even though I was a big schoolkid, my family was still the center of my world.

During my elementary school years, my family lived in these residences:

....

....

....

My parents always had time for me, although they also were busy doing these things:

....

....

....

Earlier I told you a bit about my siblings. Like most brothers and sister, sometimes we argued and sometimes we got along. Here's a bit about what we used to do together:

....

....

....

....

My childhood memories also involve uncles, aunts, cousins and grandparents. Here are some of the places we used to go and things we used to do together:

Children had chores when I was a youngster. I was expected to do these jobs:

Cooking, sewing and needlework, gardening, home repair, and automobile repair: Young people of my generation learned many skills in the home. I learned these skills from my parents:

_____

_____

_____

_____

_____

Times have changed! This is something that I did as a child that I'm sure that you, grandchild, have never done:

_____

_____

_____

_____

_____

Very Special Occasions

Is there anything more fun than holidays and celebrations? Maybe vacations!

Springtime, when warm weather returns! We celebrated these holidays in spring:

Halloween was a favorite holiday. I had great fun with friends and family:

I'll never forget the year I dressed up like this:

Our Thanksgivings were festive:

....

....

....

Christmas or Hanukkah celebrations brought the year to a joyous close:

....

....

....

I received so many special holiday gifts, but I'll never forget this one:

....

....

....

....

Family birthdays were blessed events that we celebrated like this:

One year I received a birthday present that I'll never forget:

My family also went on trips and vacations. Most people in those days traveled by car, and many trips involved seeing or visiting with relatives. My family visited these places:

We usually traveled by

We usually stayed in

I'd like to tell you a little about one trip that stands out in my mind:

Upper Grades

I thought I was really grown-up when I moved out of elementary school and into the middle grades.

In the .... grade I began attending ....

School, located in ....

The middle grades offered so many more choices for things to do—more sports, different clubs and more variety in the subjects we studied. I signed up for these sports and organizations:

....

....

....

....

I always looked forward to my favorite subject:

....

....

....

Then came the big transition—high school!

I attended .... School,

located in ....

Our school colors were .... and .... , and

we were known as the ....

In high school, I began to enjoy the following school subjects:

....

....

....

....

These special traditions were associated with my high school:

....

....

....

....

....

My activities in high school included the following sports and clubs:

Although it is hard to see yourself through someone else's eyes, I imagine that this is what my high school friends might have said about me:

Welcome To My World

Then, as now, teenagers delighted in creating their own special world.

We took great pains with our hairstyles and clothing. If you could see pictures of my friends and me in high school, you might think that we look funny, but we thought that we looked great!

Use photo corners or double-sided tape to affix photo.

These hairstyles and clothing styles were very popular with girls:

....

....

....

Guys looked cool in these hairstyles and clothing styles:

....

....

....

Yes, we had groups or cliques in high school. These were the main ones:

....

....

....

This is how I would describe the group that I belonged to:

....

....

....

....

Music rocked our world. Here's what we were listening to and dancing to:

Having a date was an exciting event! A dreamy date might involve going to one of these places:

I remember these movies that were very popular with my crowd:

These were some of our favorite movie stars:

We were also watching these programs on television:

We did some things as teenagers that I'm sure most teenagers today will never do:

You won't believe it when I tell you what some common items cost when I was a teenager:

I remember these world events that occurred during my high school years:

Family Time, Continued

Although I was becoming more independent, my family was still at the center of my life.

During my middle school and high school years, my family lived in these residences:

....

....

....

....

Here's what was going on with my parents and siblings:

....

....

....

....

....

I have precious memories of extended family members during this time:

Spiritually, I was experiencing growth and/or change in these ways:

High School Milestones

High school is a time of lots of "firsts," until senior year, when you experience a lot of "lasts."

I had had the usual grade-school flirtations and middle-school crushes, but wow! There's nothing like a person's first real girlfriend or boyfriend. Here's the story of my first "love:"

Another milestone was learning to drive. Here's who taught me and how those early lessons went:

No one ever forgets their first car! Here's what I drove:

Getting a paycheck was a thrill that I learned about on my first real job:

Those high school years really flew by. Soon it was time for the senior prom. It was a night to remember:

_____

_____

_____

_____

_____

All good things must come to an end. Here's what I remember about my high school graduation:

_____

_____

_____

_____

_____

_____

Reflections on My Growing-Up Years

Often we don't fully understand and appreciate our lives until we are looking back on them.

These are the things that my family taught me to value:

_____

_____

_____

_____

_____

My family expected me to be this kind of person:

_____

_____

_____

_____

_____

_____

A home is much more than a house. A home often becomes a little like the people who live there. This is how I would describe my childhood home(s):

_____

_____

_____

_____

_____

This is what I remember most about my mother during my growing-up years:

_____

_____

_____

_____

_____

_____

This is what I remember most about my father during my growing-up years:

As I left high school behind and looked toward adulthood, I imagined that my future would hold:

my life as an adult

Wise people know that life is what happens while you're making other plans. The vision that I had of my future didn't quite match the reality, but those twists and turns are what make life exciting.

Use photo corners or double-sided tape to affix photo.

Although I was out of high school, my education was not over. I continued to learn:

....

....

....

....

....

I also continued to grow through the jobs that I held:

....

....

....

....

....

....

....

I discovered new interests as well:

_____

_____

_____

_____

_____

I learned a lot about myself the first time I lived on my own, away from my family:

_____

_____

_____

_____

_____

_____

One of the blessings of life is finding someone to share it with. My life changed when I met the person

that you know as ....

This is how we met:

This is how I would describe the way .... looked on that day.

This is a little bit about the family that my spouse grew up in:

_____

_____

_____

_____

_____

This is a little bit about the places that were important in my spouse's life:

_____

_____

_____

_____

_____

My spouse had also been busy with schooling and jobs:

This is what I liked about the person who would become so important in my life:

We two were alike in so many ways:

....

....

....

....

....

Of course, we also had our differences:

....

....

....

....

....

We made the momentous decision to get married. Here's what I remember about the proposal:

We married when I was .... years old and my sweetheart was ....

I'd like to tell you a little bit about the big event, our wedding:

Use photo corners or
double-sided tape to affix photo.

Here's something funny that happened at the wedding:

The honeymoon is supposedly the time when married life is sweetest. Here's a little bit about the place where we spent our honeymoon:

Our early married life wasn't all sweetness and light. We were still working and learning:

We had problems and hard times to face:

But we also found time to have fun as a couple and with family and friends:

Hello, Parenthood!

Our lives together entered a new stage when we had our first child. Let me tell you a little bit about that new life and about how our lives changed.

As the years went by, we added these children to our family:

Use photo corners or
double-sided tape to affix photo.

We worked hard to make a good life for our loved ones, putting in many hours in these careers:

_____

_____

_____

Here's a little bit about the places we lived:

_____

_____

_____

_____

We shared our religious beliefs and spiritual practices with our children:

_____

_____

_____

_____

As a young family, we struggled with these problems and issues:

_____

_____

_____

_____

Our lives were not all work and no play. We loved to have fun:

_____

_____

_____

_____

Our family included pets:

_____

_____

_____

Sometimes the entire family would hit the road for a special trip or vacation:

We attended family reunions:

We loved celebrating birthdays. This is how we usually marked such occasions:

In the spring we celebrated these holidays:

In the summer we celebrated these holidays:

In the fall we celebrated these holidays:

_____

_____

_____

_____

_____

And nothing was more special than our Christmas or Hanukkah celebrations:

_____

_____

_____

_____

_____

_____

Memories of Your Parent

I know you are especially interested in what your parent was like as a child. Wouldn't it be cool if you could travel back in time and get acquainted? While you can't do that, I'll do my best to tell you about your parent as a child.

The day your parent was born was a red-letter day! Here's what I remember about that time:

_____

_____

_____

_____

Your parent's name was chosen for a special reason:

_____

_____

_____

_____

Your parent was the _____ child in a family of _____.

Here's a bit about the other children in the family:

_____

_____

_____

_____

This is how I would describe your parent as a baby:

_____

_____

_____

_____

_____

_____

Kids develop their personalities early! Here's something I remember about your parent as a toddler.

Before I could turn around, your parent was going to school. School days were fun, most of the time. Here's one of the good times I remember:

Here's one problem we had to face together:

Besides school and family, here's what your parent loved as a youngster:

_____

_____

_____

_____

_____

Before I could turn around, my child was a teenager! This is what I remember about your parent's high school years.

_____

_____

_____

_____

_____

This is how I felt when your parent left home as a young adult:

Soon, the two people that you know as your parents met and fell in love. I remember the first time I met your other parent. This is what I thought:

Use photo corners or
double-sided tape to affix photo.

Wedding bells! Your parents may have told you all about the day they married, but this is how
I remember it:

Becoming a Grandparent

The next phase of my life began when I added "grand" to "parent."

Here's how I learned I was about to be a grandparent:

_____

_____

_____

_____

I chose _____ as my grandparent name. Here's why:

_____

_____

Of course, grandchildren don't always stick to the chosen name. Here are some of the other names my grandchildren have given me:

_____

_____

_____

_____

All About You

I thought my life was full and good, but something important was missing: You!

You were my...grandchild, and this is what I remember about your birth:

_____

_____

_____

_____

Your first year of life was full of delights, and some challenges, too:

_____

_____

_____

_____

_____

_____

I could see that you had inherited these family traits:

There's nothing quite like seeing your own child become a parent. This is what impressed me about how your parents handled the responsibility of being parents:

Here's one of my favorite stories about you as a child:

We've shared so many great times, but here's one special experience that we shared:

Use photo corners or
double-sided tape to affix photo.

I love this way that you and I are alike:

....

....

....

....

....

I can see that you and I share another characteristic that can cause trouble for us:

....

....

....

....

....

....

Here's what I love most about you, grandchild:

Who's Who in Your Family

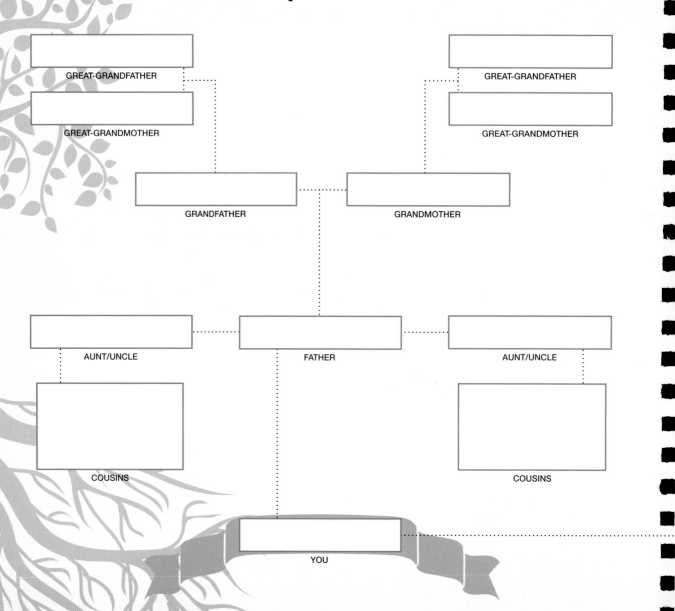

GREAT-GRANDFATHER

GREAT-GRANDMOTHER

GREAT-GRANDFATHER

GREAT-GRANDMOTHER

GRANDFATHER

GRANDMOTHER

AUNT/UNCLE

FATHER

AUNT/UNCLE

COUSINS

COUSINS

YOU

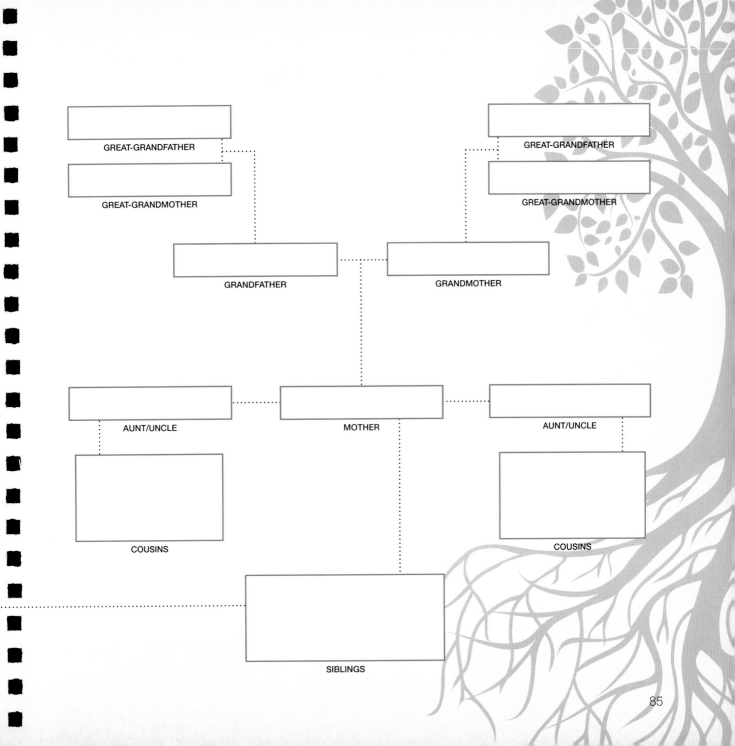

GREAT-GRANDFATHER

GREAT-GRANDMOTHER

GREAT-GRANDFATHER

GREAT-GRANDMOTHER

GRANDFATHER

GRANDMOTHER

AUNT/UNCLE

MOTHER

AUNT/UNCLE

COUSINS

COUSINS

SIBLINGS

Aunts, uncles, cousins, and more. Your early life was much enriched by your extended family. When we all get together, it can be kind of crazy! I remember these fun times we shared:

Sometimes it's hard to fit everyone into the family tree, especially when families are blended in special ways. Here are some other important people connected to you through love:

Catching Back Up With Me

I hope you enjoyed going back in time with me. Now let's talk about the present and the future.

As I write this book for you, this is what is going on in my life.

_____

_____

_____

_____

These recent events have made me very happy:

_____

_____

_____

_____

_____

These recent events have made me sad:

These are the changes that I can see coming in my life:

Becoming a grandparent was a wonderful milestone in my life, but I still have goals. Here's what I hope to accomplish in the next few years:

Here are some other milestones that I'm looking forward to:

Grandchild, I can't wait for the day that I see you do this:

Reflections

Sometimes we can't see things clearly until we are looking back upon them.

As I raised my family, these were the things that I focused upon:

These were the things that I loved most about being a parent:

These were the things that I found most difficult:

....

....

....

....

Work also helps to define our lives. The worst job I ever had was:

....

....

....

....

This is what made it so bad:

....

....

....

....

On the other hand, a job that I loved was ....
This is what I liked about it:

Some people think that growing older is a bad thing, but in some ways it is good:

However, I don't like these parts of growing older:

It can be hard to picture oneself as a grandparent. Here's how I felt at first about being a grandparent:

Although it's 99 percent good, once in a while being a grandparent can be a little difficult, too:

Here's what I love most about being a grandparent:

Here's what I love most about being a grandparent to you:

_____

_____

_____

_____

_____

I have dreams for your future:

_____

_____

_____

_____

_____

_____

Just About Me

Sometimes people don't get around to asking the questions that will help us understand each other better, but you don't have to ask. I'll tell you some things that you may not know about your grandparent!

We'll start with some little things, because little things mean a lot. I really like these colors:

My favorite foods have changed a lot through the years, but here are the ones I'm loving right now:

You may not know the name of my favorite fragrance:

You probably don't know that my favorite painting is this one:

A poem that I love to read or recite is:

These are the books and authors that have influenced me or have given me a lot of joy:

It can be hard to pick all-time favorites, but these movies are on my list:

Music has enriched many of my days. Here's what I hear playing on the soundtrack of my life:

I also have some favorite hymns or songs that I find spiritual:

As a grandparent, I've seen lots of fitness fads come and go. I tried out quite a few:

Overall, I've found that this activity is the best way for me to stay in shape:

This is how I would describe my fashion style:

I've had quite a few cars over the years, but this one was my favorite:

Collecting is a hobby that many people enjoy. Here are some of the items I've enjoyed collecting over the years:

Laughter has been such an important part of my life. Here are some of the things and people who have made me laugh:

_____

_____

_____

I've been lucky enough to have many wonderful friends in my life. I'll tell you about one and what makes that friend special:

_____

_____

_____

_____

_____

_____

_____

Would you like to know about my favorite place in the whole world?

_____

_____

_____

_____

_____

And some of my other favorite places?

_____

_____

_____

_____

_____

_____

_____

Yes, I have a bucket list of things I still want to do and places I still want to go. Here's what's on it:

As Times Change

The changes I've seen would fill up a large book, but let's talk about just a few.

This change may be the most important one I have witnessed in my life:

....

....

....

....

Wars and conflicts between nations have occurred throughout history. These are the ones that occurred during my lifetime and how they impacted my life:

....

....

....

....

....

I'll never forget where I was and what I was doing when these landmark events occurred:

In these ways, I believe the world is better today than when I was a child:

But I think there are other ways in which the world today is not as good as it was in my youth:

....

....

....

....

Some inventions that I believe have changed our lives for the good are:

....

....

....

....

I would be just as happy, however, if these had never been invented:

....

....

....

....

....

If I could make one change in the world, this is what it would be:

Grandchild, you have opportunities that I never had. If I were young today, this is what I would like to do:

What Matters to Me

If you really want to understand a person, you have to go the extra mile and learn about their deepest beliefs.

I've met many people who have inspired me to live a better life. Some of them were friends and family. Here are a few and what I admired most about them:

_____

_____

_____

_____

Some are people whom I have never met, but whom I admire just the same:

_____

_____

_____

_____

_____

If you want to understand me, you'll have to know a little bit about my political beliefs.

You'll understand even more if you know something about my religious and spiritual beliefs:

This is one spiritual value that I hope that you will embrace in your life, grandchild:

You'll know a little more about me when you read some of my favorite quotations:

Here's how I would describe the legacy that I would like to leave for my family:

_____

_____

_____

_____

_____

Here is one last bit of advice:

_____

_____

_____

_____

_____

_____

And always remember: I love you!

About the Author

Susan Adcox is a former English and journalism teacher with a degree in literature from the University of Houston - Clear Lake. For more than five years she has been the Guide to Grandparents on About.com, where she writes about topics ranging from grandparents' rights to board games for kids. She and her husband Ronnie are approaching their 50th anniversary. They have three children and seven grandchildren.

ISBN: 978-1-4403–3285-2

Other Family Tree Books are available from your local bookstore and online suppliers.
For more genealogy resources, visit **<shopfamilytree.com>**.

18 17 16 15 14   5 4 3 2 1

DISTRIBUTED IN CANADA BY FRASER DIRECT

100 Armstrong Avenue

Georgetown, Ontario, Canada L7G 5S4

Tel: (905) 877-4411

DISTRIBUTED IN THE U.K. AND EUROPE BY

F&W Media International, LTD

Brunel House, Forde Close,

Newton Abbot, TQ12 4PU, UK

Tel: (44) 1626 323200

Fax (44) 1626 323319

E-mail: enquiries@fwmedia.com

DISTRIBUTED IN AUSTRALIA BY CAPRICORN LINK

P.O. Box 704, S. Windsor, NSW 2756 Australia

Tel: (02) 4560-1600

Fax: (02) 4577-5288

E-mail: books@capricornlink.com.au

PUBLISHER/EDITORIAL DIRECTOR: Allison Dolan

EDITOR: Jacqueline Musser

DESIGNER: Geoffrey Raker

PRODUCTION COORDINATOR: Debbie Thomas

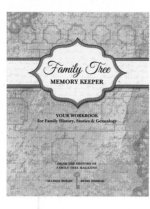